Famous Friends:

Helen Keller

AND

Mark Twain

*How They Met, Their Humble Beginnings
and Amazing Achievements*

Philip Wolny

CURIOUS
FOX
BOOKS

ABOUT THE AUTHOR: Philip Wolny is an author and editor born in Poland, and he has lived in New York City on and off since the age of four. His nonfiction titles for young-adult readers include books about US history, international politics, culture, religion, and many other topics.

© 2024 by Curious Fox Books™, an imprint of Fox Chapel Publishing Company, Inc., 903 Square Street, Mount Joy, PA 17552.

Famous Friends: Helen Keller and Mark Twain is a revision of *Famous Friends: True Tales of Friendship: Helen Keller and Mark Twain*, published in 2020 by Purple Toad Publishing, Inc. Reproduction of its contents is strictly prohibited without written permission from the rights holder.

PUBLISHER'S NOTE: This story has not been authorized by the estates of Helen Keller or Mark Twain.

Paperback ISBN 979-8-89094-010-0
Hardcover ISBN 979-8-89094-011-7

Library of Congress Control Number: 2023952480

To learn more about the other great books from Fox Chapel Publishing, or to find a retailer near you, call toll-free 800-457-9112 or visit us at *www.FoxChapelPublishing.com*.

We are always looking for talented authors. To submit an idea, please send a brief inquiry to acquisitions@foxchapelpublishing.com.

Fox Chapel Publishing makes every effort to use environmentally friendly paper for printing.

Printed in China

CONTENTS

Chapter 1
A Winter Visit 5

Chapter 2
American Author 11

Chapter 3
Light from the Darkness 19

Chapter 4
A Meeting of Minds 27

Chapter 5
A Lifetime of Friendship 33

Chronology 40

Chapter Notes 42

Further Reading 44

Glossary 46

Index 48

Their life stories may have been very different, but in some ways, Mark Twain (left) and Helen Keller (right), were more alike than not. The two loved books, laughter, and social justice.

A Winter Visit

On a cold winter's day in January 1909, four guests were on their way to meet one of America's most famous writers. One of the guests was also a famous writer and political activist.

Helen Keller was still only 28 years old, but she had lived enough for a few lifetimes already. Born in 1880, Keller fell ill with either meningitis or scarlet fever when she was just 19 months old. The sickness passed but left her blind and deaf. In the nineteenth century, people who were blind or deaf had it much harder than they do in modern times. Keller had gone on not only to overcome her disabilities, but to go to college and write books. Her story inspired millions around the world, including others who were deaf or blind.

Mark Twain, whose real name was Samuel Clemens, was a little more than a year from the end of his life. Twain was born in 1835 in Florida, Missouri. He had written two of the most popular novels in American history, *The Adventures of Tom Sawyer* and its sequel, *The Adventures of Huckleberry Finn*. His wife, Olivia "Livy" Langdon Clemens, had passed away in 1904, while two of his four children, Langdon and Susy, had died from illnesses decades before. In some ways, Keller had become another

Susy Clemens, the author's daughter, is shown in 1885.

daughter and protégé to Clemens—that is, he taught her and helped her in her career.

Keller had recently finished her latest book, *The World I Live In,* and had sent a copy to Twain. She added an inscription, or note at the beginning of the book, that read, "Dear Mr. Clemens, come live in my world a little while. –Helen Keller."[1] His answer was to invite Keller and her friends to his world.

Now, they were visiting Twain at his home in Redding where he had planned to retire for good, the mansion known as Stormfield. Keller later told how Twain's horse-drawn carriage arrived at the train station to pick them up. "[T]here was a light snow upon the Connecticut hills. It was a glorious five-mile drive to Stormfield; little icicles hung from the edges of the leaves and there was a tang in the air of cedar and pine."[2]

A path that leads up to Stormfield, Twain's Connecticut home.

As always, Keller was traveling with her companion and longtime teacher, Anne Sullivan. Anne's husband, John Albert Macy, also came along. Anne had helped teach Helen many things, and the two were almost never

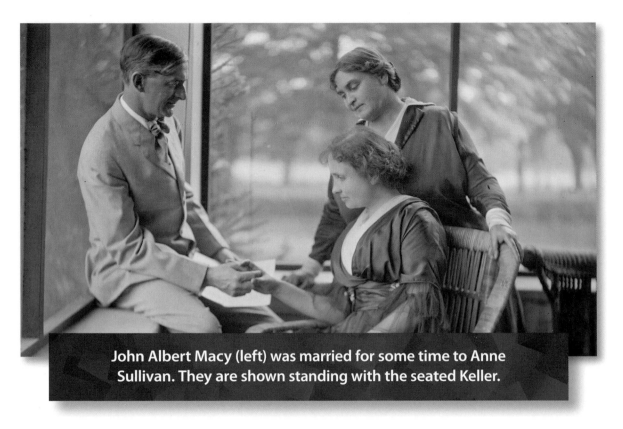

John Albert Macy (left) was married for some time to Anne Sullivan. They are shown standing with the seated Keller.

apart. Anne escorted Helen and helped her communicate, among many other tasks.

Many who learn about the friendship between Twain and Keller are pleasantly surprised. Consider also how naturally the friendship flowed from who Twain and Keller were. From her earliest memories, Keller had been forced to express herself through words instead of through sight and sound. She learned so much about the world and herself through books and, just as importantly, through the words those around her said. Because she was forced to develop her other senses—like smell, taste, and touch—she also learned more about her environment and surroundings in those ways than many people who could see and hear.

During this last meeting, as she later wrote, Keller noticed so many details and felt them strongly. These included the smells of food and the fire keeping them all warm. Twain had long been impressed with Keller's sharp senses. Wherever she was, she could tell if many books were around from the smell of their leather bindings. Even if he hadn't said a word, Keller could often tell if Twain was in a room. Twain smoked 10 to over 20 cigars a day, and their very strong scent often followed him.

Twain was a good and generous host. His guests toured the house, with Twain describing it for Anne. Anne would then "translate" for Keller by using her hands to signal the words on Keller's hands, a system sometimes known as fingerspelling. They would use the same system on their last night when they all sat down by the fireplace to hear Twain read them one of his short stories.

Throughout her life, people were fascinated by how Keller communicated.

As Twain neared the end of one of his tales, both he and the Macys saw that Keller was moved by the story—it made her cry. This ability to appreciate writing and other art drew Twain to Keller.

Twain and Keller both told stories in their own special ways. Her tales were about overcoming the limitations she was dealt. Her work helped others see people with disabilities in new ways— as people with abilities and dreams, instead of as helpless or as a burden. Twain's work spoke to Americans in different ways. His stories helped them laugh and contained messages and morals about society.

The smells and feel of nature delighted Keller as much as those of the study and library.

This 1905 portrait of the author hangs in the Mark
Twain Library, located in Redding, Connecticut.

American Author 2

Few writers are as well known or as beloved in American history as Mark Twain. He was born Samuel Langhorne Clemens on November 30, 1835. He came into the world in Florida, Missouri. At the time, Missouri was still part of the US frontier. When he was four, his family moved about thirty miles away, to Hannibal, Missouri.

Hannibal was a busy and exciting place for a young boy. The town lay on the mighty Mississippi River, which was very important to trade and business in that region. Samuel's father, John Marshall Clemens, was both a judge and a lawyer, and he ran a general store in town. He even helped organize the Hannibal and St. Joseph Railroad, which connected Hannibal to St. Joseph, at the time Missouri's second biggest town.

Many of the characters and situations Samuel later wrote about were inspired by children, events, and places he knew as a boy. He had a good memory, and he seemed to notice everything. Hannibal was later his model for the town of St. Petersburg, where the fictional Tom Sawyer and his friends lived. Even at an early age, Sam also had the independent streak many of his stories' characters had. He defied authority the first

This 1850 image is the earliest known of young Samuel Clemens. It is a daguerreotype, an early kind of photograph. Clemens wears a printer's cap.

day of school, and was punished by the teacher.

Sam's father died from pneumonia in 1847. By then, the boy had worked making deliveries and running the register at his father's store. Sam was just 11, but the following year he left the fifth grade (few people had a high school education at the time). He then became an apprentice, or helper, at a local newspaper. He learned how to set type. It was his early newspaper experiences that first opened up a world of words to the youthful Sam. He absorbed different writing styles, new vocabulary, and most importantly, new ideas and creativity.

In 1852, when he was just 16, his first piece of writing was published. "The Dandy Frightening the Squatter" ran in a sportsmen's magazine from Boston, Massachusetts, called *The Carpet-Bag*. That year, he also decided to travel and find his fortune. It was a time of great change in America, and there were many opportunities for ambitious people. He used his printing skills to land jobs in Chicago, Illinois; St. Louis, Missouri; New York, New York; and other places. For a time he lived with his brother,

Orion Clemens, in Iowa. Orion would later become secretary of the Nevada Territory during the US Civil War.

Samuel worked as a pilot on a Mississippi River steamboat during these pre-war years. He would later describe many of the things he saw in his books. River life also inspired his pen name, or pseudonym (a name used on one's writing). The word *twain* means "two." On the river, it means the water is two fathoms deep; a fathom is six feet. When the depth was two fathoms, or twelve feet, it was deep enough to float the boat safely. The boatman would shout, "mark twain."

In June 1858, Samuel's other brother, Henry Clemens, died when the steamboat *Pennsylvania* exploded. Samuel always partly blamed himself, because Henry had started pilot training after Samuel suggested he try it.

By 1861, the Civil War had begun. Sam was against slavery. In 1862, with war raging in the south and east, Sam and Orion traveled two weeks by stagecoach to Utah and then Nevada. In Virginia City, Nevada, after some misadventures in mining and a few hustles, Sam became a reporter with the town's newspaper, *The Territorial Enterprise*. He first used Mark Twain as a byline (the name one signs to one's articles)

This sculpture of Samuel Clemens as a riverboat pilot stands at Glascock's Landing in Hannibal, Missouri.

for a travel piece on February 3, 1863. No one knew it then, but a legend was born that day. Soon, people would know him better as Mark Twain than as Samuel Clemens.

Journalism and writing would become Twain's main job from then on. He was also a humorist. This meant he wrote in a funny and interesting way that made people think differently about important subjects. He

Mark Twain lived enough to fill five lifetimes— and hundreds of books.

reported from Hawaii for the *Sacramento Daily Union* of Sacramento, California. Readers loved his amusing stories.

The publication *Alta California* hired Twain to write letters reporting about life from such locations, such as Key West, Florida; California; New York City; St. Louis; and Nicaragua, among others. In 1867, another paper paid him to write about parts of Europe and the Middle East. On that trip, a passenger named Charles Langdon showed Twain a picture of Langdon's sister, Olivia, or Livy. Twain often said it was love at first sight—he was hooked, just from seeing that picture.

He communicated with Livy Langdon by letter, and they eventually met and married. Her family introduced Clemens to writers, activists, and others who wanted to change the world for the better. This suited him. He was always curious about new people, places, and things. To Twain, each person was like a new book or story to experience. From 1869 to 1871, he and Livy lived in Buffalo, New York, where Twain edited and wrote for a paper he part-owned, the *Buffalo Express*. Their son Langdon was born in 1870 but passed away two years later.

This photo shows Olivia Langdon in her early 20s, around the time that she would marry Twain.

Between 1872 and 1880, the couple had three daughters: Susy, Clara, and Jean. They then built a home in Hartford, Connecticut.

There, Twain wrote the works that made him a legend. One was the 1881 book, *The Prince and the Pauper,* which told a tale of two boys, one

A scene from *The Prince and the Pauper*. This story of characters switching places would inspire dozens of other books in the future.

rich and one poor, who switch places because they look alike. Also, *The Atlantic Monthly* published Twain's stories about river steamboat life. These would be reprinted later as a book, *Life on the Mississippi* (1883).

But Twain's most famous books are household names for American children and adults alike. The first is *The Adventures of Tom Sawyer* (1876). Many of its details came straight from Twain's childhood, including sidekick character Huckleberry Finn. Finn is the hero of the book's sequel, *The Adventures of Huckleberry Finn* (1884). It is based on a boy from

Hannibal named Tom Blankenship, who was four years older than Twain. In his autobiography, Twain described the boy: "In *Huckleberry Finn*, I have drawn Tom Blankenship as he was. He was ignorant, unwashed, insufficiently fed; but he had as good a heart as ever any boy had."[1] These two characters, and their friend Becky Thatcher, would become a permanent part of American history and culture.

A statue representing characters Huckleberry Finn (left) and Tom Sawyer (right) stands not far from Twain's childhood home in Hannibal.

Eight-year-old Helen with Anne Sullivan during a vacation to Brewster, on Cape Cod, Massachusetts, in 1888.

Light from the Darkness

On June 27, 1880, a little girl was born to Arthur H. Keller and his wife, Kate Adams Keller, in Tuscumbia, Alabama. No one could have predicted the illness (either scarlet fever or meningitis) that visited Helen Keller when she was just 19 months old. When the fever finally cooled, the Kellers realized their daughter had gone blind and deaf.

In the nineteenth century, it was even harder to grow up with a disability than now. There were fewer opportunities for people to live normal lives, become educated, or get jobs. The Kellers could have easily just kept Helen isolated, which was a common practice. Instead, they hired a teacher to help her. Anne Sullivan had suffered an eye disease at age five that had left her partially blind. She had just graduated from the Perkins School for the Blind, and at age 20 she became six-year-old Helen's governess, or teacher.

Sullivan helped Helen learn by using special techniques and languages. She used her hands to make signs on Helen's hands. She taught her that all things have names, and words have meanings. Helen was very independent, and she would sometimes start fights with her

By 1904, Helen was enjoying life's simple pleasures, like the scent of a flower and a good book to read in Braille.

teacher and her parents. She had so much anger and frustration about feeling closed off from the world, she would often throw tantrums. But Anne never gave up, and neither did Helen. Once they got used to each other, and Helen began to trust Anne, Helen's ability to learn shone through. She learned hundreds of words. Once she started, she became a lifelong lover of learning. She learned Braille, the language of raised symbols that can be read by touch. Another teacher, Sarah Fuller, helped Helen learn how to speak.

In 1888, Helen had made so much progress, her story was making her famous. That May, Helen, Anne, and Helen's mother visited Washington, D.C., to meet President Grover Cleveland. Her parents worked to get her into the Perkins School for the Blind in Boston, Massachusetts. The Kellers were not wealthy, but they had connections to many powerful and famous people. Many of them were very impressed with how hard Helen worked. They helped Keller attend the Wright-Humason School for the Deaf.

There, she could work more closely on speech, and educate herself despite her difficulties. Helen learned to read and write. She could even type by age 10. New worlds opened up to her, and Helen dreamed big.

Keller and Sullivan relocated to New York to attend the Wright-Humason School. At the end of the nineteenth century, many women never went to college, or even finished formal schooling of any kind. But Helen wanted to go to Radcliffe College in Boston.

She got her wish in 1900. She still needed the help of Anne Sullivan, who attended school with her to assist her in following lectures, writing papers, and helping with everyday tasks, just as she had at the Kellers' home. The long and lonely years of hard work would pay off. Keller's story had attracted attention, and her wit, intelligence, and sincerity attracted

Keller wears her cap during her graduation from Radcliffe in 1904.

even more. When she finished Radcliffe with honors in 1904, she was the first deaf-blind person to ever finish college.

Some members of the public were suspicious of Helen's accomplishments. She had written a short story called "The King of Frost" when she was 12, and sent it to the head of the Perkins School, Michael Anagnos. He had published it in *The Mentor,* a magazine for alumni, or former students. Some accused her of plagiarism—that is, they believed she had copied the story from elsewhere. It had similar passages and events to another well-known story published before.

In the end, Anagnos and others who supported Keller and Sullivan faced off against some teachers and school staff who wanted Keller removed from the Perkins School. They squeaked by. Anagnos cast the tie-breaking vote. Her supporters agreed with Keller that she had probably heard the original story years ago and had simply forgotten it existed.

Keller was an optimist, which meant that she had bright hopes for the future and for how things would turn out. Her attitude helped give her energy, which she would definitely need. She dedicated the rest of her life to helping both deaf

A love of nature and animals came easily to Keller.

As with Mark Twain, Keller enjoyed the friendship of the inventor Alexander Graham Bell. Bell was one of the first to see her potential.

and blind people especially, but also to change the world for the better, whatever the cause.

The world would learn much more about her through her autobiography, *The Story of My Life*. It came out in 1903, a year before she graduated from Radcliffe. It was dedicated to Alexander Graham Bell. Bell had invented the telephone and other devices, and he had communicated with his deaf mother since he was 12 years old. He spent his life fighting for deaf education. Along with Twain and others, Bell also helped support Keller by

Her disabilities did not keep Keller from the simple pleasures in life, like feeding swans. If anything, they made her enjoy them more.

introducing her to important people, and by helping pay for her education and activities.

In one passage from her book, Keller wrote, "Knowledge is happiness, because to have knowledge—broad, deep knowledge—is to know true ends from false, and lofty [high] things from low."[1] Books were her friends; they accepted her without judgment.

Keller published another important work in 1908, *The World I Live In*. This time, beyond just writing about her life, she wrote about the ways she used the senses she did have, how Anne Sullivan and others helped her, and about other tools she used to navigate daily life.

The books made her popular, and many people wanted to see the famous and brave Keller tell her story in person. She toured the nation, and traveled overseas, to keep pushing for deaf and blind people—and all people—to get the education and opportunities they wanted. Keller would often tell crowds how being curious and having an imagination were the greatest gifts life had given her. So were the ability and desire to help others.

Her first public speaking event occurred in 1913. Even though she technically could neither see nor hear the audience that came to her lecture in Montclair, New Jersey, she knew there would be a crowd. She later wrote that she nearly panicked in the moment. However, she ended up doing just fine, and went on to give hundreds of speeches.

A 1913 portrait of Keller and Sullivan show how the two women had grown older together.

Keller, Sullivan, and Twain pose for a picture with Laurence Hutton, a famous publisher who took an interest in helping Keller.

CHAPTER

A Meeting of
Minds

4

From 1894 to 1896, Keller attended the Wright-Humason School for the Deaf in New York City. She attended many events and met many important and famous people who were interested in her life and inspirational story.

One day, she attended a party at the house of a well known magazine editor, Laurence Hutton. He had set up the event to introduce Keller, then 14 years old, to other people. One of the guests was none other than Mark Twain. He was 58. Back then, most people did not live as long as they do now, but Twain was still full of energy and good humor. On the other hand, he had money problems, because he had invested in many inventions and schemes. Some were successful, but others were total failures. His youngest daughter, Jean, was the same age as Helen. It is possible Helen reminded him of Jean, which helped them connect the way they did.

As always, Anne was traveling with Helen. The other guests were waiting for them when they first entered Hutton's library. Keller's sharpened senses—probably her sense of smell in particular—helped her figure out that she was surrounded by hundreds of books. The leather they were bound in and the smell of the paper gave them away.

Hutton's guests were curious about how Keller communicated. Sullivan had taught her to "feel" the words of a speaker by holding her fingers up to his or her lips. Helen showed them how by shaking hands with the other guests and feeling Sullivan's lips as she said their names out loud. Sullivan told Keller that Twain looked like the famous Polish composer Jan Paderewski.

Famous novelist William Dean Howells was there, and Keller agreed to demonstrate with him. Howells told a long story. Twain thought he could

Another guest that met Keller was the American author and critic William Dean Howells.

see "each detail of it pass into her mind and strike fire there and throw the flash of it into her face."[1] Soon enough, Twain told a story to Keller the same way. He was thrilled at how she knew where to ask questions (through Anne Sullivan), and how she chuckled and burst into laughter at certain points in the stories.

She even spoke, though her words were rough and broken. Sullivan asked her what Twain was known for, and Keller answered, "For his humor . . . and for his wisdom," just as Sullivan said the same thing.[2] Keller had been handed a bouquet of flowers when she arrived at Hutton's house. She took one flower from it and put

"MARK TWAIN,"
AMERICA'S BEST HUMORIST.

As one of the most respected and recognizable Americans, Twain was often the subject of cartoons, too.

it in a buttonhole on Twain's jacket. Keller later said she felt like they had become instant friends.

Twain made Keller laugh with his stories. He knew about her life and difficulties, but he did not put her on the spot with pity or concern. Many blind and deaf people, and others with disabilities, feel sad or upset when others treat them differently, as if they are helpless or strange. Keller had

Twain seems to take a moment to think a line or word over. The author's curious and questioning mind was similar to Keller's.

others ask her if she was sad, or if life without sight or sound was boring or frightening.

Keller experienced none of that with Twain. Instead, he treated her as an equal. This made Keller happy, especially since she was a young woman. Even though people saw teenagers differently then—more as adults than children—young women often struggled for respect.

In one of Keller's later books, Twain was quoted on his attitude toward Keller and blindness in general. Speaking with someone who thought that

Keller must have a sad and lonely life, Twain reportedly said, half-joking, "You're wrong there; blindness is an exciting business, I tell you. If you don't believe it, get up some dark night on the wrong side of your bed when the house is on fire and try to find the door."[3]

The old author saw the excitement and interest with which Keller approached everything in the world. She loved to learn, from books and from people she met. This quality inspired Twain and made them fast friends. Twain was famous for being sarcastic and critical, but Keller saw beyond the rough edges of his humor.

Soon after they met, Twain was so excited about making friends with Keller that he started to help her in any way he could. He was friends with many important and wealthy people, and he hoped they could help Keller in her education.

Keller and Twain met many more times. Over the years, as Keller said, "He knew . . . many things about me; how it felt to be blind and not be able to keep up with swift ones. . . . He never made me feel that my opinions were worthless. He knew that we do not think with eyes and ears, and that our capacity for thought is not measured by five senses."[4]

The author tries out a light at the lab of inventor Nikola Tesla.

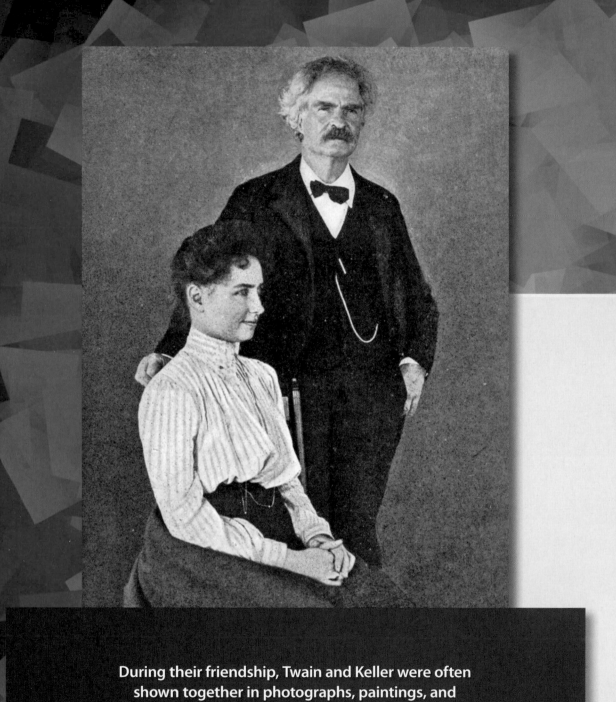

During their friendship, Twain and Keller were often shown together in photographs, paintings, and illustrations in magazines and newspapers.

A Lifetime of Friendship

Like some of the fictional people in his books, both Twain and his new friend Keller were colorful. People wanted to hear about them, for many different reasons. According to biographer Amy Chambliss, Twain thought Keller was one of the two most interesting people of the nineteenth century. The other was the famous French general and emperor, Napoleon Bonaparte. Twain was also one of the most interesting and exciting people Keller had ever heard about, much less met.

After their visit, Keller's time in New York ended. She went back to Boston, where she entered the Cambridge School for Young Ladies. Four years later, she entered Radcliffe College. These opportunities might not have been possible without her friendship with Twain. Money was always hard to come by. The family needed it not just for Keller's education, but also to pay for a home, food, and other expenses for Keller and for Sullivan.

In 1896, Twain wrote to Emelie Hart, the wife of Henry Rogers. As the head of Standard Oil, Rogers was one of the richest men in the world. He had advised Twain on his business dealings before. He seemed a good bet for someone whose great wealth could help Keller.

Oil man Henry Rogers used his great wealth for many charitable purposes, including helping with Keller's education and well-being.

Twain wrote about how well prepared for college she was. To waste the young woman's potential would be almost a crime, he insisted. According to Chambliss, Twain said, "It won't do for America to allow this marvelous child to retire from [end] her studies because of poverty. If she can go on with them she will make a fame that will endure in history for centuries."[1]

Both Twain and Keller were overjoyed when Rogers agreed to sponsor her through her studies. In addition, when Twain was around, he would keep a close eye on those around her. He made sure they were looking out for her best interests.

Keller and Twain met again in 1901. By then, Anne Sullivan had begun a relationship with John Albert Macy. Macy was a Harvard University teacher and book critic, and later he would work as Keller's editor and manager. He accompanied the two women to see their old friend Twain in mid-January. Of the meeting, Twain wrote in his autobiography, "I had not met her for a long time. In the meantime, she has become a woman."[2] It wasn't only that Keller was now an adult in college. The things she had learned, not just from books but about herself and her situation, had helped her grow up.

At the same time, Keller was becoming more like Twain. He had written about many of the things he thought were wrong with the world, especially in America.

Keller became a well-known speaker, often talking about the issues facing people who were blind, deaf, or otherwise facing a disability. She fought for their rights and became a symbol of others' struggles. Fighting for them helped her meet other people who wanted to change the world for the better.

During the winter of 1903, Twain read Keller's autobiography, *The Story of My Life*. He was curious about her story, and reading it helped cheer him

Toward the end of his life, Twain's wife's failing health often depressed him.

up. Livy was sick and he feared she did not have long to live. Twain had also suffered illness. And he was growing old.

In 1904, on the advice of doctors, his family moved to Italy for its warm and sunny weather. There, Livy passed away. Twain wrote a letter to Keller, saying, among other things, "I am charmed with your book—enchanted. You are a wonderful creature, the most wonderful in the world—you and your other half together—Miss Sullivan."[3]

As good a friend as she had in Twain, Keller's one irreplaceable companion was Anne Sullivan.

She enjoyed the praise, and wrote back to thank him and comfort him in his time of need. "Do try to reach through grief and feel the pressure of [Livy's] hand, as I reach through darkness and feel the smile on my friends' lips and the light in their eyes though mine are closed."[4]

Livy's death seemed to take much of the life out of Twain. He never stopped complaining about people and how they were often mean, greedy, selfish, or otherwise unpleasant. He also never lost his affection for many of the people he had met over the years. He was still thrilled to have Keller's company. He

Twain's immediate family pictured left to right: daughters Clara, Jean, wife Olivia, and daughter Susy.

also loved to hear about her progress in life, whether in person with Anne translating, or through news stories.

The feeling was mutual for Keller. Most of Twain's writing was behind him. For Keller, it was just beginning. In 1908, she published *The World I Live In*. It continued the story of her life, adding more of how she was able to experience life and talk with others. Reading the book inspired Twain to invite Keller and Sullivan to visit. He realized that it might be the last time. He was over 70 years old.

Their visit at Stormfield lasted for three days. Her favorite part of it was the last night, when Twain read her his story "Eve's Diary." The story was inspired by his wife's death, and was written shortly after it. As he finished

Few can deny that Twain is among the most famous American writers.

reading, an emotional Keller teared up.

It would indeed be their last meeting. Twain predicted that the passing of Halley's Comet, which happened every few decades, would bring his own death. He had been born the same year as the comet's earlier appearance in 1835. After some poor health, it seemed he was ready to make good on that prediction. He passed away from a heart attack on April 21, 1910. He was 74 years old.

Among many other experiences, Keller's friendship with Twain would continue to affect her. She dedicated herself to improving others' lives. America had growing industries that were making many people rich. Others worked hard, for long hours and little money. Their health suffered, and many workers lived in very poor conditions.

Keller joined other reformers: people who wanted to change, or reform, things to make work and life easier for others. One thing she fought for was women's suffrage—that is, their right to vote, which women still lacked at the time. She also was a pacifist, a person who is against war and violence. Not many people know that she joined the American Socialist Party in 1908. Her political beliefs were tied to her beliefs about helping others, and for having people in society help each other.

She also gained fame as a lecturer. Keller would hardly slow down over the next five decades as a speaker, writer, and activist. The American Foundation for the Blind made Keller their spokesperson in 1924. She set records for fundraising. Her example also inspired others to start groups. Rather than let the world get her down, she would

Keller's work took her worldwide. Here, she visits Japan in 1948 as a Goodwill Ambassador for the US government.

do something about it. Keller reportedly told the *New York Tribune* in 1916, "For a time I was depressed . . . but little by little my confidence came back and I realized the wonder is not that the conditions are so bad, but that humanity has advanced so far in spite of them. And now I am in the fight to change things."[5]

By the time she suffered some heart troubles and retired for good, it was 1961. She lived the rest of her years at home. She passed away in her sleep on June 1, 1968. One can imagine that Twain would have been happy. She had led a long, productive, and inspiring life that influenced millions. Keller might have felt the same about Twain. In the end, it was a once-in-a-lifetime meeting of hearts, minds, and souls.

1835	Samuel Langhorne Clemens is born on November 30 in Florida, Missouri.
1839	The Clemens family moves to Hannibal, Missouri, a town that will inspire many of his later works.
1847	Sam's father dies of pneumonia. Sam is just eleven.
1848–52	Finishing any sort of formal schooling, the young Clemens works as a printer's apprentice, writer, and editor.
1857–1859	Clemens earns his steamboat license while working on the Mississippi River.
1861	Clemens leaves for Nevada with his brother, Orion Clemens, who will become Secretary of the Nevada Territory before it becomes a state.
1863–1866	Clemens becomes a reporter and signs his stories Mark Twain. He reports on events in California, Hawaii, and elsewhere.
1867	Twain travels to Europe, the Middle East, and elsewhere. He works as a secretary to Nebraska Senator William Stewart. His first book, the short story collection, *The Celebrated Jumping Frog of Calaveras County, and Other Sketches*, is published.
1870	Twain marries Olivia Langdon, settling first in Buffalo, New York. They move to Hartford, Connecticut. Their son Langdon is born and dies two years later.
1876	One of Twain's most important books, *The Adventures of Tom Sawyer*, is published.
1880	Helen Keller is born on June 27 in Tuscumbia, Alabama.
1881	Twain publishes *The Prince and the Pauper*.
1882	Helen suffers the sickness that will claim her eyesight and hearing.
1883	*Life on the Mississippi* is published.
1884	Twain's book, *The Adventures of Huckleberry Finn*, is published.
1886	Alexander Graham Bell and Helen Keller meet for the first time.
1887	Anne Sullivan begins her lifelong role as a teacher and companion to Keller.

1891–1894 The Clemens Family moves to Europe for a time to escape debt problems.

1894 Moving to New York, Helen attends the Wright-Humason school. She meets Mark Twain at a party.

1896 Captain Arthur Keller, Helens' father, passes away.
The Clemens' daughter Susy dies.

1903 Keller's autobiography, *The Story of My Life*, is published. She also published her book, *Optimism*, the same year.

1904 Keller graduates with honors from Radcliffe College. She is the first deaf and blind person to get a college degree. Keller buys a house in Wrentham, Massachusetts.
Olivia Clemens dies.

1906 The Massachuetts Commssion for the Blind appoints Keller to its board.

1908 Keller publishes *The World I Live In*, sharing more of her story with the world.

1909 Twain's daughter Jean suffers a seizure and drowns in the bathtub.

1910 Twain dies at Stormfield on April 21.

1921 Kate Keller, Helen's mother, dies.

1924 The American Foundation for the Blind makes Keller its spokesperson.

1927 Keller publishes *My Religion*.

1929 She publishes *Midstream: My Later Life*.

1946 Keller starts a series of world tours to advocate for the disabled, especially the blind and deaf. Because of Keller's efforts, many nations and groups establish schools for the blind and deaf.

1964 President Lyndon B. Johnson awards Keller the Presidential Medal of Freedom for her lifetime of activism.

1968 Keller passes away peacefully in her sleep in Easton, Connecticut.

Chapter 1. A Winter Visit

1. "Mark Twain and Helen Keller," Mark Twain Stormfield Project, March 2013, http://twainproject.blogspot.com/2012/03/mark-twain-and-helen-keller.html?m=1
2. Gary Scharnhorst (editor), *Twain in His Own Time* (Iowa City: University of Iowa Press, 2009), pp. 310–311.

Chapter 2. American Author

1. Geoffrey C. Ward and Dayton Duncan, *Mark Twain: An Illustrated Biography* (New York: Alfred A. Knopf, 2001), p. 76.

Chapter 3. Light from the Darkness

1. Helen Keller, *The Story of My Life* (New York: Penguin, 1996), p. 48.

Chapter 4. A Meeting of Minds

1. Mark Twain, *Autobiography of Mark Twain: Reader's Edition, Volume 1* (Oakland: University of California Press, 2012), p. 364.
2. Peter Carlson, "Encounter: Helen Keller Touches Mark Twain's Heart," *American History*, August 7, 2017, https://www.historynet.com/encounter-helen-keller-touches-mark-twains-heart/
3. Helen Keller, *Midstream: My Later Life* (Charleston, SC: Nabu Press, 2011), p. 115.
4. Amy Chambliss, "The Friendship of Helen Keller and Mark Twain," *The Georgia Review*, Vol. 24, No. 3 (Fall 1970), p. 305.

Chapter 5. A Lifetime of Friendship

1. Amy Chambliss, "The Friendship of Helen Keller and Mark Twain," *The Georgia Review*, Vol. 24, No. 3 (Fall 1970), p. 308.

5. Mark Twain, *Autobiography of Mark Twain, Volume 2: The Complete and Authoritative Edition* (Oakland: University of California Press, 2013), p. 167.

6. Jon Jones, "Mark Twain & Helen Keller's Special Friendship," *Openculture.com*, May 13, 2015, https://www.openculture.com/2015/05/mark-twain-helen-kellers-special-friendship.html

7. Ibid.

8. Barbara Bindley, "Interview with Helen Keller," *New York Tribune*, January 16, 1916.

Books

Ashmore, Wayne, and Jennifer Nault. *Mark Twain*. New York: AV2/Weigl, 2015.

Bodden, Valerie. *Mark Twain*. Minneapolis, MN: ABDO Publishing, 2013.

Garrett, Leslie. *Helen Keller*. London, UK: DK Publishing, 2013.

Maloof, Torrey. *The World of Mark Twain*. Huntington Beach, CA: Teacher Created Materials, 2017.

Mattern, Joanne. *Helen Keller*. New York: Children's Press/Scholastic, Inc., 2015.

Shores, Erika L. *Helen Keller*. North Mankato, MN: Capstone Press, 2014.

Works Consulted

"Ask Keller—July 2007." American Foundation for the Blind.

Blakemore, Erin. "History's Other Odd Couple: Mark Twain and Helen Keller." *Daily JStor*, March 4, 2015. https://daily.jstor.org/historys-odd-couple-mark-twain-helen-keller/

Carlson, Peter. "Encounter: Helen Keller Touches Mark Twain's Heart." *American History*, August 7, 2017, https://www.historynet.com/encounter-helen-keller-touches-mark-twains-heart/

Chambliss, Amy. "The Friendship of Helen Keller and Mark Twain." *The Georgia Review*, Vol. 24, No. 3 (Fall 1970), pp. 305–310.

Jones, Jon. "Mark Twain & Helen Keller's Special Friendship." *Openculture.com*, May 13, 2015. https://www.openculture.com/2015/05/mark-twain-helen-kellers-special-friendship.html

Keller, Helen. "My Friend Mark Twain." *Mark Twain Journal*, Spring/Summer 1958, p. 1. Retrieved December 20, 2018. https://www.jstor.org/stable/42656545?mag=historys-odd-couple-mark-twain-helenkeller&seq=1#metadata_info_tab_contents

Keller, Helen. *The World I Live In*. New York: New York Review of Books Classics, 2015.

Morris, Roy, Jr. *American Vandal: Mark Twain Abroad*. Cambridge, MA: Belknap Press/Harvard University Press, 2015.

Twain, Mark. *Autobiography of Mark Twain: Reader's Edition, Volume 1*. Oakland: University of California Press, 2012.

Twain, Mark. *Autobiography of Mark Twain, Volume 2: The Complete and Authoritative Edition*. Oakland: University of California Press, 2013.

Wheeler, Jill C. *Mark Twain*. Edina, MN: ABDO Publishing, 1996.

On the Internet

American Foundation for the Blind (AFB)
https://www.afb.org/

Helen Keller International
https://www.hki.org/

apprentice (uh-PREN-tis)—A helper or assistant who works under a more experienced person to learn about a job or profession.

binding (BYN-ding)—The material or fabric that holds the pages of a book together, and usually covers the front and back of the book.

Confederate (kun-FEH-dor-it)—Relating to the group of states that fought to leave the United States in the Civil War.

confidence (KON-fih-dents)—A feeling of trust and belief in oneself and that one's actions will be successful.

daguerreotype (duh-GAYR-oh-typ)—An early type of photograph produced on silver.

fingerspelling (FING-er-spel-ing)—A type of sign language in which the fingers are used to form letters to spell out words.

frontier (frun-TEER)—A place on the border of a known area; an unknown or unexplored area.

fundraising (FUND-ray-zing)—The process of asking others to give money to help a worthwhile cause or person.

hustle (HUH-sul)—A dishonest way to make money.

inscription (in-SKRIP-shun)—Something written at the beginning of a book to send a message or to mark the book as a gift.

lecture (LEK-shur)—Prepared, spoken words delivered at a meeting, a class, or other gathering.

meningitis (men-in-JY-tis)—An infection of areas around the brain and human spine that causes fever, headache, and sometimes confusion or death.

optimist (OP-tih-mist)—A person who has a positive outlook about the future and how things will turn out.

plagiarism (PLAY-jur-ism)—The act of copying the work of another person and claiming it as one's own.

protégé (PROH-teh-zhay)—A person trained or helped by another person who is usually older and more successful, especially when it comes to his or her career.

reformer (ree-FOR-mer)—A person who works to help change, or reform, things in society in a way that will help people.

scarlet fever (SKAR-let FEE-ver)—A disease caused by bacteria that brings on fever and a red, or scarlet, rash, usually affecting children.

sequel (SEE-kwul)—A book that continues the story of a previous one.

steamboat (STEEM-boht)—A type of boat or ship common in the nineteenth century that used hot steam power to move itself on water.

Adventures of Huckleberry Finn, The (novel) 5, 16–17, 40
Adventures of Tom Sawyer, The (novel) 5, 11, 16–17, 40
Anagnos, Michael 22

Boston 12, 21, 33
Braille 20
Buffalo Express (newspaper) 15

Carpet-Bag, The (newspaper) 12
Civil War, US 13, 46
Clemens, Clara (daughter) 15, 37
Clemens, Henry (brother) 13
Clemens, Jean (daughter) 15, 27, 37, 41
Clemens, John Marshall (father) 11–12
Clemens, Langdon (son) 5, 15, 40
Clemens, Olivia "Livy" (wife) 5, 14–15, 36–37, 40–41
Clemens, Orion (brother) 12–13, 40
Clemens, Samuel (*see also* Twain, Mark) 5, 11–14, 40
Clemens, Susy (daughter) 5–6, 15, 37, 41
Cleveland, Grover 21

daguerreotype 12, 46

"Eve's Diary" 37

Florida, Missouri 5, 11, 40
Fuller, Sarah 20

Halley's Comet 38
Hannibal, Missouri 11, 13, 17, 40
Hartford, Connecticut 15, 40
Howells, William Dean 28
Hutton, Laurence 26–29

Keller, Helen
    birth 5, 19, 40
    death 39, 41
    education 19–23
    family 19–21
    as lecturer 25, 39
    and plagiarism 22, 46
"King of Frost, The" 22

Life on the Mississippi (novel) 16

Macy, John Albert 34
Mississippi River 11, 13, 40

Perkins School for the Blind 19, 21–22
Prince and the Pauper, The (novel) 16, 40

Radcliffe College 21, 33, 41
Rogers, Henry 33–34

Sacramento Daily Union, The (newspaper) 14
Story of My Life, The 23, 35, 41
Stormfield 6, 37, 41
Sullivan, Anne 6–8, 17–18, 20–22, 24–29, 33–34, 36–37, 40

Territorial Enterprise, The (newspaper) 13
Tesla, Nikola 31
Twain, Mark (born Samuel Clemens)
    birth 11, 40
    death 38, 40
    education 12
    family 5, 6, 11–15, 35–37, 40–41

World I Live In, The 6, 24, 37, 41
Wright-Humason School for the Deaf 21, 27, 41